VIKING COOKBOOK

SFG

Contents

Food and drink in the Viking era

Introduction
Tom Bloch-Nakkerud

[York AY23 The Viking Household]
Vikings are known to have settled and built farms and villages in many of the countries they travelled to. Archaeological digs in York, England – the Vikings' Jorvik – have provided us with extensive knowledge of their way of life. At the Jorvik Viking Centre in York, parts of a Viking village have been reconstructed in full scale; the photo illustrates the preparations for the evening meal.

[UO C4321 Hylestad stave church portal, detail: Sigurd roasting the dragon's heart]
Both food and drink were important elements of Viking cultural events. The legend of Sigurd who killed the dragon is older than the Vikings. Just over a century after the Viking Age, this legend was depicted in the portal of Hylestad stave church in Setesdal. In the final scene, we can see Sigurd roasting the dragon's heart, using his sword as a roasting spit.

VIKINGS! Some thousand years ago, this cry would have triggered panic and flight. The Vikings' reputation was well-known and feared – voyagers sailing from the coast of Scandinavia and crossing the North Sea to other coasts. Their vessels were open and could be powered by both oar and sail. Nowhere seemed safe from these intrepid voyagers. The first lands to suffer their plundering were Britain and the Continent. Later, the Vikings found their way upstream along the rivers, extending their voyages far into Europe. If they found something to plunder, they would help themselves. Resistance was no obstacle to the Vikings. They would sail out again, their wake red with blood and the village they had just plundered a smouldering fire…

This depiction of these Scandinavian barbarians is an endorsement of the popular Viking myth and reputation. But thanks to a more elaborate study of source material, and not least to the results of numerous archaeological digs, we now have a much fuller picture of the Viking era.

In the home of the Vikings, what is now Norway, Sweden and Denmark, life was very civilised. After 300 generations of trial and error, the Vikings had managed to adapt their way of life to the Scandinavian climate and environment. People lived on farms, where they kept farm animals and worked the land. They also went fishing and hunting, and their cuisine was in fact highly developed. Take the words of Odin, the greatest of the Viking gods, as he described Viking hospitality:

[The Bayeux tapestry]
William the Conqueror, on winning
the Battle of Hastings in 1066,
took England as his prize. He was Duke
of Normandy and a descendant of the
Viking chieftain, Rollo, count of Rouen
and the surrounding land. The Battle
of Hastings was depicted as a "cartoon
strip" on a 70-metre long tapestry which
is now on exihibition in Bayeux, France.
The extract above illustrates the banquet
before the battle. To the right of the two
cooks working over the pot hanging over
the fire, we can see the baker taking hot
bread from a kind of oven.
In the next scene, the cooks carry spit-
roast birds still on the spit to the table.
A horn is blown: the banquet is ready,
the food is served, the bishop blesses
the food, on his right we can see
William the Conqueror helping himself,
then they all set about eating.

Food and clothes
are needed for the man
who has travelled the mountains.
Water and towels
he can expect
when he is invited to the table.

As a host, your generosity knew no
bounds, and you piled your table high
with both food and drink. But as a
guest, you ate and drank your mead with
moderation – neither too much nor too
little.

The Germanic people in Scandinavia
had used writing in the form of runes
since the third century AD. Through
contact with the Romans, they became
familiar with the Roman alphabet, and
this formed the basis for the further
development of the runic alphabet.
The characters were made up of straight
lines, as these were easier to carve into
wood with a knife. However, most of the
Runic writings preserved today were
carved onto rune stones – inscribed with
eulogies and erected as memorials to
friends or relatives.

The art of poetry was highly valued in
the Viking era. It was deemed so
important that kings and chieftains
engaged their own poets, so-called
skalds, who would immortalise their
masters' fame and reputation in verse.
The *skalds* also wrote songs about the
gods, epic poems and words of wisdom.
Poetry was an integral part of the Viking
culture. It was not preserved in writing,
but was sung or recited, and some of this
oral tradition was passed on from
generation to generation.

Most artisan crafts were so highly
advanced by the Viking Age that they
had become specialist trades. For
example, people had been smelting iron
from bog iron ore for a thousand years.
Blacksmiths had developed refined
techniques for forging the cutting edge
of swords from harder steel than the rest
of the sword. This allowed them to make
the cutting edge even sharper while the
sword remained reasonably flexible.

Objects made of textiles, wood, glass,
stone and precious metals which have
been found have such a highly artistic
quality that they were almost certainly
created by professional craftsmen.
Handicrafts and works of art were also
traded and brought home from long

[Silver figure of a lady, ATA / Statens
Historiska Museum 128]
The lady depicted on this piece of silver
jewellery from Öland in Sweden is
holding out a drinking horn. This image
can also be found in Viking Age stone
carvings, where the hero is handed a
drinking horn by a Valkyrie on arriving
at Valhalla.

voyages. In terms of volume, commodities such as salt were most important. The Scandinavians traded furs, iron and dried fish for these goods.

At the beginning of the Viking era, trade between the countries bordering the North Sea had already been going on for centuries. With the Vikings came their ships – a decisive new factor. Previously, the only ships built were powered by oar alone. But after a long period of development of both keel and hull, the Viking seafarers could at last hoist rigging and sails. This literally opened up a whole new world of opportunity. The Vikings set sail, they discovered new lands: first Iceland, then Greenland, then Vinland, later known as America.

On Viking farms, only cows and bulls could be termed farm animals. Sheep and goats roamed free all year round, and pigs were only kept indoors during the winter in the coldest parts of Scandinavia. The Stone Age farmer was the first to tame the wild boar. From then on, the pig became smaller and lighter. Its slaughter weight was between 30 and 40 kg – the modern pig is twice as heavy when slaughtered. One lamb provided 5 kg of meat, compared with 15–20 kg today. Other animals on Viking farms were ducks, geese and hens, and dogs and cats.

On the land, the Viking farmer grew the same types of corn farmed today. Their main tool was the ridging hook, an iron hook pulled by a horse or a bull to dig a furrow in the soil. The greatest progress made in agriculture was when the ridging hook was replaced by the plough. This new tool turned up the soil, creating larger fields and resulting in greater harvests. Vegetables and herbs were readily available, growing wild, and roots, nuts, fruit and berries were gathered from a great variety of plants.

The elk and bear were the most common game, followed by wild boar, roedeer, red deer and reindeer. The Vikings dug pits to catch elk and reindeer. The pits were covered with branches and moss and built so that the animals could not climb back out once they had fallen in. The Vikings hunted with bows and arrows and spears.

Eilif Elg carried fish to the Raudsjøen Lake. This inscription was found on a rune on the Li farm in Gausdal. It tells us of the Vikings' attempts to help Mother Nature. Carrying fish, most often trout, involved releasing fish into a watercourse with no fish stock. In the case of Eilif Elg, he carried fish to a lake 711 metres above sea level. The primary purpose of the inscription was probably to establish the farm's right to that fish. The Vikings fished with spears, nets, fish

[UO C27997B]
Soapstone is a relatively soft stone and can be whittled with a knife. It is therefore perfect for making pans. The Norse word for stone is grjot, the first form of the modern words **gryte,** or pan, and **grøt,** the porridge cooked in the pan. In Norway, soapstone became even more popular than earthenware, and soapstone was exported. However, in southern Scandinavia, earthenware was more common.

spears and fishing lines with hooks. They also used fishing nets and fish traps. According to the season, they fished along the coast, in the rivers and mountain lakes. The fish was dried or smoked to preserve it, so that the inland villages could enjoy the fruits of the seasonal fishing along the coast.

The Scandinavian coast provided its inhabitants with a rich and varied diet: firstly the sea with seal and whale and plenty of seabirds and eggs; then the countryside with all its game and plant life.

The main meals were eaten in the morning and evening, the so-called *dagverd* and *nattverd*. In Viking houses, the fireplace was open and situated in the middle of the floor. There was an opening in the roof for the smoke from the fire. The cooking pot hung over the fire, unless that day's meal was to be fried or spit-roasted. Both meat and fish were placed in clay pots to roast, just as we use foil today.

[UO Oseberg 1412. Neg/dia 24177]
The Oseberg ship contained the richest collection of Viking kitchen utensils ever found, fit for a queen. Here are a number of wooden objects for the table: oblong dish, ladle, bowl and knife.

During the winter, the most common meat was boiled pork. The Vikings ate mutton and beef all year round. Goat was the least valued meat, while veal roasted whole was kept for festive occasions. After slaughtering sheep, the Vikings enjoyed charcoal-grilled sheep's head. Horsemeat was kept for the sacrificial festivals in the autumn, winter and spring. Bear meat was the most popular game, followed by hare and woodland birds.

Flour was probably not used in large quantities, judging by the method used to grind corn – it was ground by hand. The dough did not rise, but was baked as flatbread on an iron pan or stone slab. The dough consisted of flour, milk, water and salt.

The Vikings did not eat from plates and they had no forks. But everyone had their own sheath knife, and wooden or bone spoons. Porridge and soups were either eaten from one big pan, or served in wooden cups.

The most common drinks were water, milk and juice made from berries and plants. Beer was brewed from corn with malt and hops. It was served with meals, and known as *munngodt*.

The longer it was left to ferment, the higher the alcohol content and the Vikings had fun drinking their *gammelt øl*, or old beer. They made mead by adding honey to the beer.

Increasing trade with Europe saw the introduction of wine from the Rhine and Mosel regions to the Viking table, initially only for royals and chieftains.

We have compiled this book of recipes in the hope that it will bring the reader to a closer understanding of the Viking era, through food and meals. It contains some fifty recipes, ranging from simple, plain fare to festive meals with several courses complete with beverages. We are sure you and your guests will really enjoy a genuine and delicious taste of Viking life.

Good luck and bon appetit!

[UO C24176-A-C O.1383]
When the Vikings went ashore to prepare their meals, they brought with them an iron pot which stood on its own stand over the fire. This particular pot holds 35 litres and was found on the Oseberg ship.

hIC FECERVN: PRANDIVM:

[Roasting spit and baking iron,
Historisk Museum, Bergen]
The roasting spit, shaped like a fork in
this illustration, had a wooden handle.
However, on the baking irons for baking
round bread, the handles were also
made of iron – these would get very hot
and you had to protect your hands
before picking them up from the heat.
Top: Extract from the Bayeux Tapestry.

NETTLE SOUP

serves 4

1 ½ – 2 l young nettles
1 l vegetable stock
3 tablespoons flour
100 ml milk or cream
salt, white or black pepper
½ – 1 teaspoon chervil or thyme
4 eggs

Rinse and blanch the nettles.
Drain the nettles. Bring the
vegetable stock to the boil.
Add the nettles. Add the flour
mixed to a paste with a little cold
water, and boil for several minutes
until slightly thickened. Add the
milk or cream. Season with salt,
pepper and chervil or thyme.
Hard-boil the eggs and peel them,
then halve them. Place two egg
halves in each soup bowl.

RUSSIAN BEETROOT SOUP

serves 4 – 6

5 – 6 beetroot
water
1 teaspoon salt per litre water
approx. 300 g cabbage
2 onions
2 tablespoons butter
1 ½ l stock
salt
½ teaspoon cumin
50 ml chopped parsley

Brush and rinse the beetroot,
keeping a little of the root and top.
Place them in lightly salted boiling
water and boil until soft (approx.
30 – 40 minutes). Drain and leave
to cool.

Peel and shred the beetroot. Shred
the cabbage and onion and fry in
the butter.
Add the stock and simmer for
approx. 15 minutes. Add the
beetroot and bring to the boil.
Season with salt, pepper and cumin.
Garnish with the chopped parsley.
Serve with soured cream and bread.

Soups

*Delicious, nutritious soups have
traditionally been an important
part of the day-to-day diet. And a
good soup has always been popular
on the menu at festive meals.*

*There are many kinds of onion
growing wild in Scandinavia.
The most common is the forest
onion, known as* kajplök *in
Gotland. This onion tastes rather
like leek and is delicious sliced in
various dishes, particularly soups
and salads, adding a fresh,
spicy flavour.*

Another wild onion is the
ramslök. *During the spring, it gives
off an intense onion scent which
attracts walkers in the forest.
Its leaves have a wonderful taste
reminiscent of both garlic and
onion, and it can be used finely
chopped in all kinds of dishes.*

*Swedish Vikings were known as
Russians along the eastern trade
routes where trading stations were
set up. These later grew into the
towns and cities of modern – day
Russia.*

FOREST ONION SOUP

serves 4

500 ml forest onions
500 ml water
2 tablespoons butter
1 ½ pinches of freshly ground
black pepper
1 sprig of thyme
200 ml vegetable stock
150 ml milk
150 ml cream
2 tablespoons flour
salt

Rinse and slice the onions.
Bring the water to the boil, add the
onions and bring back to the boil.
Add the butter, seasoning and
stock. Add the milk and cream.
Mix the flour to a paste with a little
milk and add to thicken.
Bring the soup back to the boil.
Season with salt and serve with
freshly baked bread.

CABBAGE SOUP

serves 4

a half cabbage
2 carrots
2 parsnips
2 beetroot
2 onions
1.2 l vegetable stock
1 teaspoon thyme
1 bay leaf
4 whole cloves
50 ml chopped parsley
50 ml soured cream

Finely shred the cabbage, clean and grate the carrots, parsnips and beetroot, peel and chop the onion. Place all the vegetables in a pan, pour over the stock and season. Boil for approx. 15 minutes. Sprinkle with parsley and top with the soured cream immediately before serving. Serve with freshly baked bread.

CARROT STEW

serves 4

8 carrots
2 onions
1 cooking apple
200 g mushrooms
150 g bacon
300 ml stock
1 pinch of freshly ground black pepper
100 ml parsley, finely chopped
butter

Peel and thinly slice the carrots. Peel and chop the onion. Clean the mushrooms and chop in large pieces. Shred the bacon and fry until crispy. Fry the onion and carrots in the bacon fat. Place the onions and carrots in a pan and pour over the stock. Cover and boil for approx. 5 minutes. Core and chop the apple in large pieces, then fry with the mushrooms in some butter. Add with the bacon to the pan. Season with pepper and parsley. Serve with freshly baked bread.

SPINACH SOUP

serves 4

100 – 150 g fresh, blanched spinach or approx. 200 g frozen spinach leaves
1 leek
1 l stock
100 ml parsley, finely chopped
1 pinch of pepper
½ pinch of ginger

TO SERVE
2 – 3 egg yolks
100 ml whipping cream
grated nutmeg

Rinse and clean the fresh spinach or defrost the frozen leaves and chop. Thinly slice the white part of the leek and rinse well. Bring the stock to the boil and add the spinach and leek. Boil for approx. 5 minutes. Add the parsley and boil for a few minutes more. Season with salt, pepper and ginger. Whisk the egg yolks with the cream in each soup bowl. Pour the soup over while whisking. Grate a little nutmeg over each bowl and serve with fresh bread.

Fish

FRIED BALTIC HERRING
serves 4

1 kg Baltic herring, whole
100 ml dark rye flour
1 teaspoon salt
1 pinch of white or black pepper
2 tablespoons butter

Gut and clean the fish, leaving the backbone. Rinse thoroughly under running water and drain. Mix the flour with the salt and pepper. Coat both sides of the fish in the flour mixture. Fry in butter over a medium heat until the herring browns and is cooked right the way through, about 3 – 5 minutes on each side. This recipe can also be made using herring fillets. Serve the herring with cranberry sauce

SPLIT HERRING
serves 4

1 kg fresh herring
salt
butter

Gut, clean and split the herring, leaving the head intact. Rinse under running water, sprinkle with plenty of salt and leave for about 2 hours. Pierce the fish through the head with sharp sticks and hang them to dry in strong sunshine for about 8 hours. When dried, fry the herring in butter. Serve with cranberry sauce.

Since time immemorial, herring has been part of the staple diet in coastal villages. Today, it is often served as a special delicacy in Scandinavia.

To the north of Kalmarsund, the Baltic herring in its vast shoals is known as strömming *and to the south as* sill. *The Baltic herring is slightly smaller than its North Sea relative, but both types of herring can be prepared in the same way.*

A medium fatty fish perfect for frying, salting, marinating and smoking.

Pike and perch are among the more common of our freshwater fish. They are also caught in the brackish water of the Baltic Sea, where the pike and perch tend to be much larger.

The Vikings had to wait until the salmon swam upstream to spawn, before they could go salmon fishing. Today, you can buy farmed salmon all year round.

SALTED AND GRILLED HERRING
serves 4

1 kg whole Baltic herring
1 l water
100 ml salt
1 tablespoon butter

DILL BUTTER
50 g butter
50 ml dill, finely chopped

Gut and clean the fish, leaving the backbone. Rinse thoroughly under running water and drain. Mix the water and salt in a bowl. Place the herring in the salty water and leave for 1 hour. Remove the herring and drain well. Fry over a strong heat for 2 – 3 minutes on each side or grill over charcoal. If you prefer to grill it, place the herring on a grid, brush with butter and grill for 2 – 3 minutes on each side.
Serve the herring while hot with dill butter and bread.

CHARCOAL-GRILLED PERCH

serves 4

1 kg perch
2 teaspoons salt
1 pinch of white or black pepper

HERB BUTTER

4 tablespoons butter
50 ml dill, finely chopped
50 ml parsley, finely chopped
1 tablespoon chopped chives

Gut and thoroughly clean the fish. Sprinkle with salt and pepper both inside and outside. Mix the butter with the herbs. Stuff the fish with the herb butter. Grill the fish over charcoal, 8 – 12 minutes on each side, depending on thickness. Serve with bread.

PIKE AND HORSERADISH

serves 4

1 pike, about 1 ¼ kg
1 ½ – 2 teaspoons salt
parsley

Preheat the oven to 175°C. Gut and clean the pike. Do not remove the head but remove the gills. You do not need to scale the fish as the skin is removed when serving. Grease a small roasting tin or ovenproof dish. Salt the inside of the fish and stuff with parsley stalks. Place the fish in the tin/dish and roast until the flesh is white and firm and separates easily, approx. 40 minutes. Make a cut along the backbone and pull off the skin. Sprinkle lots of parsley over the fish stock in the tin. Serve the pike with melted butter, finely grated horseradish and boiled root vegetables.

PAN-FRIED COD

serves 4

700g cod fillet or one whole cod, approx. 1 kg
3 tablespoons butter
150 ml parsley, finely chopped
2 teaspoons salt
(½ teaspoon finely grated nutmeg)

Cut the fish into 2 cm thick portions. Alternatively you can prepare the fish whole. Leave the fish to soak in cold water. Grease a shallow, wide pan and sprinkle a layer of parsley on the base of the pan. Place the fish or fish portions on top of the parsley, making sure they do not overlap. Sprinkle with salt and grated nutmeg (optional) and the rest of the parsley. Place knobs of butter on top of the fish and cover. Cook the fish over a very low heat until it feels firm, approx. 20 – 30 minutes. If the fish is whole, turn after 10 – 15 minutes. Serve with boiled root vegetables.

NORWEGIAN COD

serves 4

500 g cod fillet
2 tablespoons salt
1 l water
50 g butter
1 packet bacon, approx. 140 g

Cut the fish into 2 cm thick portions. Bring the water and salt to the boil in a large pan. Place the fish in the water and simmer over a very low heat until white and firm, approx. 5 minutes. Drain the fish and dot with butter. Fry the bacon until crispy. Drain off the fat on kitchen paper. Sprinkle the bacon over the fish. Serve with boiled root vegetables.

GRILLED SALMON STEAKS

serves 4

4 salmon steaks (about 2 cm thick)
1 – 2 tablespoons butter
1 teaspoon salt

GAME BUTTER

50 g butter
6 crushed juniper berries
50 ml chopped chives

Pat the fish slices dry. Mix the ingredients for the game butter and put to chill. Grill the salmon for 3 – 4 minutes on each side, then salt. Serve with the game butter, grilled leeks and lightly boiled vegetables.

Meat

ROAST PORK WITH CLOVES

serves 6 – 8

1 kg fresh pork with rind
1 teaspoon salt
2 pinches of white pepper
10 – 15 whole cloves

Preheat the oven to 175°C.
Take a sharp knife and cut through
the rind to make a diamond pattern.
Sprinkle with salt and pepper.
Place the pork with the rind up in a
roasting tin or ovenproof dish.
Stick the cloves into the rind.
Roast for 1 ¾ hours, until the meat
has a temperature of 80°C. Drain off
the roasting juices and keep to one
side. Brush the rind with some of
the juices. Grill the pork at 275°C
for 2 – 5 minutes until the rind
becomes crackling. Remove the
pork from the oven.

SAUCE

400 ml roasting juices
50 ml water
2 tablespoons flour

Add water to the strained roasting
juices to make up 400 ml. Place in
a pan and bring to the boil. Mix the
flour to a paste with a little cold
water. Whisk the flour into the
stock. Boil for approx. 3 minutes.
Season to taste. Remove the
crackling and slice the pork.
Serve with the crackling, sauce and
lightly boiled vegetables.

*Farmers produced lamb and
mutton both before and after the
Viking era. Various types of strong-
tasting herbs, both wild and
cultivated, are the perfect
accompaniment to lamb.*

*Pork has long been considered
the most versatile of meats in
Scandinavian cuisine. It can be
used in numerous ways,
both for special occasions and
from day to day.*

*Game hunting is still a very
popular sport with modern
Scandinavians. For the Vikings,
it provided an essential source
of food.*

PORK AND APPLE

serves 4

400 g fresh or lightly salted pork,
sliced
1 teaspoon butter
2 onions
2 – 3 apples
1 tablespoon pork dripping or
butter
1 pinch of white or black pepper
2 – 3 whole cloves

Peel and slice the onions.
Core and slice the apples.
Fry the pork over a medium heat.
Turn 2 – 3 times. The longer you
fry it, the crispier the pork. Fry the
onion and apple slices in the
dripping or butter over a low heat
until they brown and soften.
Layer the pork, onion and apple
slices in the frying pan and heat
through. Season with pepper and
cloves.Serve with freshly baked
bread.

ROAST LAMB WITH MINT

serves 6 – 8

1 leg of lamb on the bone,
1 ½ – 2 kg

MINT BUTTER

50 g butter
1 teaspoon salt
1 pinch of black pepper
50 ml chopped parsley
1 clove crushed garlic or *ramslök*
1 teaspoon dried mint
50 ml breadcrumbs

Preheat the oven to 175°C. Trim the leg of lamb. Place in a roasting tin or ovenproof dish. Make the mint butter and spread it over the lamb. Roast for 1 ½ – 2 hours, until the meat has a temperature of 70 – 75°C. Remove the lamb from the oven and leave to rest.

SAUCE

roasting juices
300 ml stock
200 ml whipping cream
mint
salt, pepper

Add 300 ml water or stock to the juices and bring to the boil. Stir in the cream and simmer over a low heat for approx. 10 minutes. Season with the mint, salt and pepper. Thinly slice the lamb. Serve with the sauce, fried onion and carrot and swede rosti (see recipe on page 29).

ROAST LAMB WITH HORSE-RADISH AND HERB SAUCE

serves 8

1 leg of lamb on the bone,
1 ½ – 2 kg
2 teaspoons salt
2 pinches of coarsely ground black pepper
2 teaspoons rosemary

HORSERADISH BUTTER

3 tablespoons butter
3 tablespoons grated fresh horseradish

Start by preparing the horseradish butter. Mix the butter and the horseradish. Shape into a small sausage shape and place in the freezer until hard. Make several deep cuts in the lamb. Stuff slices of the horseradish butter into the cuts. Rub the lamb with salt, pepper and rosemary. Roast in an oven preheated to 175°C. Roast for 1 ½ – 2 hours, until the meat has a temperature of 70 – 75°C.

SAUCE

500 ml roasting juices and stock
3 tablespoons flour
200 ml whipping cream
100 ml chopped parsley
2 tablespoons chopped fresh chervil or 2 teaspoons dried chervil
salt and black pepper
3 – 4 tablespoons finely grated fresh horseradish

Strain the roasting juices and add stock to make 500 ml liquid. Mix the flour to a paste with the cream. Whisk the flour and cream paste into the stock. Add the herbs. Boil gently for approx. 5 minutes. Season with salt, pepper and grated horseradish. Thinly slice the meat. Serve with the sauce and boiled vegetables.

ROAST WILD BOAR WITH BILBERRY SAUCE

serves 6

approx. 1 kg wild boar
butter
2 onions
2 carrots
1 piece of fresh ginger
2 tablespoons honey
salt and pepper
200 ml stock

Brown the meat on all sides in a
frying pan then place in a large pan.
Peel and slice the onions and
carrots. Add the onion, carrots,
ginger, honey and stock to the pan.
Cover and simmer over a low heat
for approx. 1 hour or until the meat
reaches a temperature of 75°C.

BILBERRY SAUCE

500 ml juices from meat
100 ml whipping cream
3 tablespoons flour
100 ml bilberries
1 tablespoon grated ginger
salt and pepper

Strain and measure the juices.
Add stock if required to make up
500 ml. Add the cream and bring
to the boil. Mix the flour to a paste
with a little cold water and
whisk into the stock. Boil for
3 – 5 minutes. Carefully stir in the
bilberries. Season with ginger,
salt and pepper. Slice the wild boar.
Serve with honey-glazed root
vegetables (see recipe on page 29).

Game

*The Scandinavian forests had rich
stocks of game birds. Wood grouse,
black grouse and other types of
grouse provided delicious meals
for special occasions – and pigeon
was a special delicacy.*

GAME STEW

serves 4

approx. 500 g elk, roe deer or beef,
off the bone
butter
1 teaspoon salt
1 pinch of black pepper
1 bay leaf
15 crushed juniper berries
2 tablespoons chopped fresh thyme
or 2 teaspoons dried thyme
200 ml stock
4 carrots
4 parsnips
200 ml whipping cream

Cut the meat into chunks and
brown in butter. Place in a large
pan. Add salt, pepper and herbs.
Pour over the stock, cover and
simmer over a low heat for
1 – 1 ½ hours. In the meantime, peel
the carrots and parsnips.
Cut into small pieces and fry in a
little butter. Place them in the pan
and pour over the cream.
Cover once more and simmer for
approx. 15 minutes. Season with
salt and pepper.

Garnish with fresh thyme.
Serve with freshly baked bread.

ROAST GROUSE ON A BED OF REDCURRANT

serves 4

2 grouse, plucked, singed and cleaned
butter
1 ½ teaspoons salt
½ teaspoon white pepper
200 ml stock

Truss each bird to give an even shape. Brown the birds on all sides in a frying pan. Salt and season and pour over a little stock. Cover and simmer until the meat feels tender – test it with a sharp object. This should take approx. 50 minutes. Remove the birds and keep them hot.

SAUCE

300 ml grouse juices or stock
50 ml concentrated redcurrant juice
2 tablespoons flour
100 ml whipping cream
1 teaspoon thyme
salt and pepper
300 – 400 ml redcurrants

Drain the juices and add stock to make up 300 ml. Bring to the boil. Add the redcurrant juice.
Mix the flour to a paste with a little cold water and whisk into the liquid. Add the cream and boil for 3 – 5 minutes. Season with thyme, salt and pepper. Slice the meat and serve on a bed of redcurrants with sauce and boiled vegetables.

NORMANDY PIGEON WITH CIDER SAUCE

serves 4

4 pigeons
½ teaspoon salt
1 pinch of white pepper
2 carrots
75 g celeriac
1 leek
1 onion
butter
500 ml chicken stock
500 ml cider
1 pinch of thyme
2 bay leaves
200 ml whipping cream
1 apple

With a sharp knife, carefully remove the breast fillets from the pigeons and keep to one side. Cut up the rest of the carcass. Peel and chop the carrots, celeriac, leek and onion. Brown the carcass in butter in a frying pan. Add salt and pepper and place in a large pan. Fry the vegetables in butter in the frying pan and place in the pan. Pour over the stock and cider, add the herbs and boil for approx. 40 minutes. Strain the stock and remove the scum. Bring back to the boil and reduce by 50%. Add the cream and season with salt and pepper.
Chop the apple and stir it into the sauce. Fry the pigeon breasts in butter in the frying pan for approx. 5 minutes on each side. They should be slightly pink in the centre, with a temperature of 65 – 70°C. Serve the pigeon with the sauce and carrot and swede rosti (see recipe on page 29).

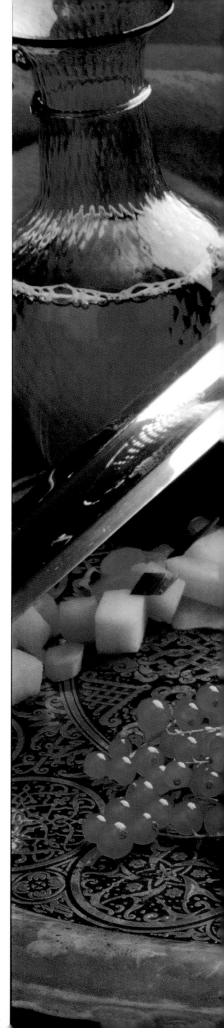

Poultry

Fowl and chicken were domestic birds, providing both meat and eggs. They varied somewhat in size, and the most common species was a little smaller than the modern fowl.

HONEY-GRILLED HERB CHICKEN

serves 4 – 5

1 chicken, about 1 ½ kg
1 teaspoon salt
1 – 2 pinches of white or black pepper
1 teaspoon ground herbs, such as chervil, tarragon or rosemary
2 tablespoons melted butter
1 tablespoon honey

Preheat the oven to 175°C. Rub the chicken both inside and outside with salt and herbs. Place the chicken in a roasting tin or ovenproof dish. Brush with melted butter and honey. Roast until the meat is tender and the juices are clear, around 1 ¼ – 1 ½ hours. Serve with creamed broad beans (see recipe page 29).

CHICKEN STEW WITH BEER

serves 4

1 chicken, approx. 1 kg
3 – 4 carrots
3 onions
1 swede, approx. 500 g
1 ½ teaspoon salt
1 pinch of black pepper
2 pinches of thyme
6 – 8 peppercorns
330 ml beer (bitter)

Divide the chicken into 8 pieces. Peel and chop the vegetables. Brown the chicken in butter for approx. 5 minutes on each side. Season with salt and pepper and place in a large pan. Add the vegetables, thyme, peppercorns and beer. Bring to the boil and simmer for approx. 15 minutes. Serve with bread.

FINNISH-STYLE GRATINATED ROOT VEGETABLES

serves 4

2 – 3 carrots, approx. 300 g
2 parsnips, approx. 300 g
3 eggs
250 ml whipping cream
1 teaspoon salt
1 pinch of black pepper
parsley

Chop the carrots and parsnips into small pieces. Boil in lightly salted water for approx. 10 minutes. Drain the vegetables, then chop finely. Add the eggs, cream, salt and pepper. Stir until you get a smooth consistency, then place in a greased tin with removable sides, about 24 cm in diameter. Bake on the lowest shelf of an oven preheated to 175°C for approx. 40 minutes. Remove the sides of the tin. Garnish with parsley and serve with smoked ham.

CARROT AND SWEDE ROSTI

serves 4

2 – 3 carrots
1 swede
1 large leek
1 ½ teaspoons salt
2 pinches of coarsely ground black pepper
butter
1 teaspoon rosemary

Peel the carrots and swede and roughly grate them. Divide the leek in two lengthways and slice thinly. Mix the carrots, swede, leek, seasoning and herbs. Heat the butter in a frying pan until light brown. Place half the mixture in the pan and fry for approx. 2 minutes. Stir once or twice then press down the mixture to flatten it out. Cover and cook for another 5 minutes until crispy. Turn the rosti and fry the other side. Remove from pan and fry the rest of the mixture in the same way.

CREAMED BROAD BEANS

serves 4

1 ½ kg broad beans in their pods, or approx. 400 g shelled beans,
2 carrots
water
1 teaspoon salt per litre water

WHITE SAUCE
2 ½ tablespoons flour
400 ml milk + vegetable stock
1 tablespoon butter
salt, pepper

Shell, de-stem and rinse the beans. Peel and slice the carrots. Boil the beans until soft in lightly salted water, approx. 30 minutes. Add the carrots after approx. 15 minutes. Mix the flour to a paste with a little of the milk in a pan. Add the rest of the milk, vegetable stock and butter. Bring to the boil, stirring constantly, then simmer for 3 – 5 minutes. Add the beans and carrots and mix carefully. Season with salt and pepper.

CREAMED VEGETABLE SOUP

serves 4

6 – 8 baby carrots, approx. 300 g
approx. 250 g mangetout
approx. 100 g fresh spinach
700 ml water
1 ½ – 2 teaspoons salt
1 tablespoon flour
500 ml milk

Rinse the vegetables and slice or chop. Boil in lightly salted water for approx. 5 minutes until just soft (start the carrots first as they take longer to cook). Mix the flour to a paste with 100 ml of the milk. Add this to the vegetables while stirring and boil for 3 - 5 minutes. Pour the rest of the milk into the pan and bring to the boil.

Vegetables

Root vegetables are the perfect accompaniment to all types of meat dishes. Even in the Viking era there was a great variety of these vegetables. Swede was considered such an important foodstuff that a number of historical Land Acts dictated that all farmers had to grow swedes on a certain portion of their land.

HONEY-GLAZED ROOT VEGETABLES

serves 4

1 swede
2 – 3 carrots
½ cabbage
1 leek
butter
honey
salt and pepper

Peel and chop the root vegetables (do not add the leek yet). Boil them in lightly salted water for approx. 5 minutes and drain. Brown the root vegetables on all sides in butter until soft. Add the leek towards the end and brown. Stir in the honey and season with salt and pepper.

MIXED ROOT VEGETABLES

serves 2

4 beetroot, approx. 200 g
2 parsnips, approx. 100 g
1 tablespoon butter
50 – 100 ml water
½ teaspoon salt
1 pinch of black pepper

Peel and dice the vegetables. Fry the vegetables quickly in a little butter. Pour over the water and season with salt and pepper. Boil for approx. 5 minutes.

Pancakes

BILBERRY PANCAKE

serves 4

250 ml flour or
100 ml graham flour + 150 ml plain
flour
½ teaspoon salt
600 ml milk
3 eggs
2 tablespoons butter
200 ml bilberries

Preheat the oven to 225°C.
Whisk the pancake batter without
the butter and stir in the bilberries.
Melt the butter in a roasting tin and
pour in the batter.
Bake on the middle shelf until the
pancake is light brown, approx.
20 – 25 minutes. Slice and serve
with jam or stewed fruit.

GRIDDLE CAKE

serves 4

100 ml flour
½ teaspoon salt
400 ml milk
5 eggs

Mix the flour and salt.
Add a little of the milk and whisk to
a smooth paste. Whisk in the rest of
the milk and the eggs. Melt a little
butter in a frying pan. Pour in the
egg mixture and cook on a medium
heat. Stick a fork or sharp object in
the mixture to test whether it is
completely firm. To turn, slide onto
a plate or lid then slide back into
the frying pan on the other side,
and cook until light brown.
Serve with fried apple slices,
stewed apple or cranberry jam.

*Pancakes are extremely versatile.
The fruits of the forest provide
a great variety of accompaniments
to pancakes, with bilberries one of
the most delicious alternatives.*

*The Gotland area has a wild
species of blue raspberry called
salmbär, which makes delicious
juice and jam. They are also very
tasty eaten fresh with a splash
of milk.*

*The Gotland pancake is a very
historic dish. No-one knows for
sure how old it is, but it is thought
to date back to the Viking era.
The most surprising ingredients are
saffron and rice, which makes you
wonder whether it can really be
that old.*

*But then think of the Vikings
on their great voyages to the East,
arriving at the bazaars of
Constantinople where the air is
filled with exotic fragrances and
colours. Naturally, they would
bring goods back to Scandinavia
from their voyages, and saffron is
so striking that you can't help but
notice it. Rice may also have been
imported in small quantities.*

SMOKED PORK PANCAKE

serves 4

½ kg smoked pork
500 ml milk
7 eggs
150 ml flour

Slice the pork and fry lightly.
Keep half the pork fat in the pan.
Whisk together the eggs, flour and
milk and pour the batter into the
hot pan. Lift and prod the batter
with a spatula from time to time to
stop it sticking to the pan. When the
pancake seems firm, slide it onto a
suitable plate. Put the pork back in
the pan, pour in some of the fat
then slide the pancake uncooked
side down back into the pan.
When the pancake is cooked, slide
it out of the pan, turning it so the
pork side is up. Serve with
cranberry jam.

SAFFRON CREAM PANCAKE

serves 4

3 egg yolks
½ g saffron
2 tablespoons honey
3 tablespoons flour
300 ml whipping cream
3 egg whites

Preheat the oven to 175°C. Mix the
egg yolks, saffron, honey and flour
together. Whisk the cream and egg
whites in two bowls. Carefully fold
the cream and the egg whites into
the saffron mixture. Pour the
mixture into a greased cake tin with
straight sides. Bake on the bottom
shelf until risen and light brown,
approx. 40 minutes. Serve the cake
with raspberry or blackberry jam.

GOTLAND PANCAKE

serves 6

150 ml pudding rice
½ teaspoon salt
2 tablespoons butter
700 ml milk
300 ml cream
200 g chopped sweet almonds
3 chopped bitter almonds
3 tablespoons honey
1 g saffron
3 eggs

Preheat the oven to 200°C.
Boil the rice in 300 ml water with
the salt. Once the water has evapo-
rated, add the butter and milk.
Then add the cream and cook for
several minutes. Stir in the almonds,
honey and saffron. Whisk the eggs
and stir in. Grease and flour a tin
and pour in the mixture. Bake for
approx. 25 minutes. Serve warm
with *salmbär* jam and lightly
whipped cream.

Fruit

CRANBERRY PEARS

approx. 600 g cranberries
300 ml water
approx. 300 ml honey
1 kg small, firm pears

Remove the stalks from the cranberries, rinse them, and place them in a large pan. Pour over the water and honey. Bring to the boil and then simmer over a low heat uncovered for approx. 10 minutes. In the meantime, peel the pears, keeping the stalk. Scrape the stalk with a knife and cut a cross over the eye. Place the pears in the pan and cook together with the cranberries until the pears are soft, approx. 30 minutes. Remove the scum. Place the cranberry pears in sterile, hot jars and pour over the syrup. Screw on the jar tops and leave to cool. Store the pears somewhere cool and dark.

CHERRY SOUP

serves 4

500 ml fresh cherries, stoned
200 ml freshly squeezed cherry juice
50 – 100 ml honey
1 cinnamon stick
600 ml water

Mix the cherries, juice, honey and cinnamon in a pan. Bring to the boil and cook for 2 minutes. Serve the soup ice cold.

Fruit and berries were in almost unlimited supply during the late summer and autumn. During this season, it was important to preserve the fruits of nature.

STEWED PLUMS

serves 4

1 kg plums
50 ml water
100 – 200 ml honey

Halve and stone the plums. Boil them in the water for approx. 5 – 10 minutes. Add the honey and stir until dissolved. Serve the stewed plums with cold milk.

BERRY JAM

approx. 1 kg raspberries or bilberries
400 ml honey

Clean and rinse the berries under running water. Place in a pan. Cover and simmer over a low heat for approx. 5 minutes. Stir in the honey. Simmer over a low heat uncovered for approx. 15 minutes. Remove the scum. Pour the jam into sterile, hot jars, filling each jar. Screw on the jar tops. Leave to cool. Store somewhere cool and dark. If you want to store the jam for long, it should be frozen.

NUT AND HONEY CAKE

12 slices

100 g hazelnuts
50 g dried apple
150 ml honey
4 eggs

Preheat the oven to 175°C.
Finely chop the hazelnuts and
apple. Mix the nuts, apple and
honey in a bowl. Whisk in the eggs.
Spread the mixture into a large
circle on a greased baking tray
(baking paper). Bake on the middle
shelf for approx. 15 minutes.

CRANBERRY AND HONEY CREAM
200 ml whipping cream
100 ml honey
200 – 300 ml cranberries

Mix the cream and honey in a pan.
Simmer the mixture while whisking
until it thickens. Stir in the
cranberries and leave to cool.
Spread the cranberry and honey
cream over the cake and serve with
whipped cream.

RHUBARB CAKE

serves 4

500 g rhubarb
50 ml honey
100 ml rolled oats
100 ml chopped hazelnuts
50 g butter
50 ml honey
2 tablespoons milk
1 tablespoon flour
cream

Preheat the oven to 225°C.
Clean and chop the rhubarb.
Place the rhubarb in a greased cake
tin. Mix the rolled oats, nuts, butter,
honey, milk and flour in a pan.
Bring to the boil stirring constantly.
Spread the mixture over the
rhubarb. Bake in the oven until
light brown, approx. 15 minutes.
Serve the rhubarb cake with
whipped cream.

Cakes

*Even the Vikings were known to
have a sweet tooth. Honey was
often used to sweeten both food
and beverages, and they used the
sweet resin of the cherry tree as a
type of chewing gum.*

HAZELNUT CAKE

CAKE DOUGH
150 g butter
100 ml honey
2 egg yolks
450 ml flour

FILLING
50 ml honey
100 g ground hazelnuts
100 ml flour
1 tablespoon cooking oil
4 eggs
2 egg whites, whisked until stiff

Preheat the oven to 175°C.
Make up the cake dough using only
400 ml of the flour. Remove one
fourth of the dough and crumble
into a bowl with the rest of the
flour. Keep to one side. Press the
rest of the dough into a cake tin,
covering the bottom and sides.
Prick the dough and leave somewhere cool. Bake the dough for
approx. 5 minutes making sure it
does not brown. Mix the nuts with
the honey, flour and oil. Whisk in
one egg at a time, then gently fold in
the egg whites. Pour the filling over
the cake dough and sprinkle the
dough crumbs on top. Bake the
cake for 40 minutes. You may have
to cover the cake with baking paper
after 20 minutes to stop it getting
too dark. Leave the cake to cool
and serve with whipped cream.

Beverages

CRANBERRY DRINK

approx. 1 l

approx. 1 kg cranberries
500 ml water
300 ml honey

Pick the stalks off the cranberries
and rinse and drain. Mash the
berries in a bowl, pour over the
water and cover well. Leave in
a cool place for 1 – 2 days.
Stir the berries several times during
this period. Strain the berries
through a jelly bag. Leave to drip for
approx. 30 minutes. Mix the juice
with the honey and remove the
scum. Pour the cranberry drink into
clean, cold bottles with screw tops
or corks. Store somewhere cool
and dark.

APPLE DRINK

7 ½ l

6 l chopped apples
6 l water
150 – 200 g honey

Put the apples in a bucket and pour
over the water. Leave for 4 days.
Drain and keep the juice.
Pour in the honey and mix until
dissolved. The apple drink can be
stored for up to one week.

ELDERFLOWER DRINK

approx. 3 l

40 elderflower heads
5 apples
wood sorrel or common sorrel
(optional)
2 l water
500 ml honey

Thoroughly rinse the flowers and
thinly slice the apples. Layer the
flowers, apples and sorrel in a large
jug or bowl. Bring the water and
honey to the boil and pour over
the flowers and apples.
Cover and leave in a cool place for
3 – 5 days. Strain the juice through
a jelly bag and pour into clean jars.
Leave to cool. Can be stored for up
to one week in the fridge.

WARRIOR'S MEAD

When brewing mead, you must make sure that all your utensils are as clean as possible. To brew around 18 l of mead, you need a stainless steel pan which holds about 25 l, a 20 l demijohn with a rubber seal and a fermentation lock, plastic tubing, gauze and a slotted ladle.

Before brewing, thoroughly clean all your utensils and containers.

INGREDIENTS
12 l cold water
6 l honey
100 ml dried rose hips
50 ml cloves
1 yeast culture

Bring the water and spices to the boil. Stir in the honey until dissolved. Simmer over a low heat for about 1 hour, continuously removing the scum. Remove the pan from the heat and leave to cool overnight. Mix the ingredients for the yeast culture and leave this to cool overnight too.

YEAST CULTURE
500 ml water
2 tablespoons sugar
½ teaspoon yeast nutrient
¼ teaspoon citric acid
wine yeast for 18 l

Once the must is lukewarm, you can add the yeast culture. Mix well, cover and stand in a warm place. When the fermentation process has just begun, quickly pour the must into a demijohn and seal with the fermentation lock and rubber seal. Leave the must to ferment in a warm place for about a week to 10 days. Strain the must and pour it back into the demijohn. Seal once more and leave in a warm place until the fermentation process is completed. This will take a further 3 – 5 weeks. Strain the must one more time and pour into bottles which can be sealed.

BALDER'S BEER

Anyone can brew their own beer, and make just as good beer as the best commercial breweries. But your efforts could also produce something undrinkable and most definitely not deserving to be called beer. The secret to success lies in the care you take during the brewing process. To brew around 25 l of beer, you need a stainless steel pan which holds approx. 25 l, a demijohn of the same size with a rubber seal and a fermentation lock, plastic tubing, gauze, a sieve and a large (approx. 30 l) plastic bucket with a tight lid and a hole in the lid for the fermentation lock.

Before brewing, thoroughly clean all your utensils and containers.

INGREDIENTS FOR THE WORT
5 l good quality water
6 kg malt extract
30 g bog myrtle

Bring the water to the boil and add the malt extract and the bog myrtle. Boil for approx. 1 hour. In the meantime, pour 10 l of cold water into the fermentation bucket. Remove the pan from the heat. Add 5 l of ice to cool the wort and stir with the sieve until the ice melts. Strain the wort into the bucket, and add more water until you have a total of approx. 25 l. When the temperature of the mixture in the bucket is around 20 – 25°C, add 2 packets of brewer's yeast. Seal the bucket with the lid and the fermentation lock. Fermentation should start after 2 – 20 hours and you should leave the wort to ferment for around 5 days before pouring it into the demijohn. Seal with the rubber seal and fermentation lock, and leave to ferment. Place the demijohn in a slightly cool place as the beer tastes better if left to ferment slowly. The fermentation process should take about 2 weeks. The beer is ready to drink when there are long intervals between the yeast bubbles. You can now pour the beer into clean bottles for storage, but it should be drunk as soon as possible.

NOTE ON MEASUREMENTS

You will find that some dry ingredients are measured by volume (ml or l) rather than by weight (g or kg). This is a Scandinavian custom. We are unfortunately unable to provide a conversion table from ml to g, as naturally the volume/weight factor will differ for each ingredient (e.g. flour weighs more than parsley). However, most kitchens are equipped with a litre measuring jug and this can be used very effectively to measure out the ingredients by the volume indicated.

Happy cooking!

PHOTOS:

pp. 4-5: Hylestad-portal, Universitetets Oldsakssamling, Oslo

p. 5: Viking Household, Jorvik Viking Centre, York

p. 6: Tapisserie de Bayeux, Centre Guillaume le Conquérant

p. 6: Silver figure, Statens Historiska Museum, Stockholm

p. 7: Pan of soapstone, Universitetets Oldsakssamling, Oslo

p. 8: Kitchen utensils, Universitetets Oldsakssamling, Oslo

p. 8: Iron pot, Universitetets Oldsakssamling, Oslo

p. 9: Tapisserie de Bayeux, Centre Guillaume le Conquérant

p. 9: Roasting spit and baking iron, Historisk Museum, Bergen

p. 3: Lennart Hansson

pp. 11-37: Lennart Hansson

pp. 38-39: Samfoto, Jørn Areklett Omre

Egmont Bøker Fredhøi AS - SFG
N-0055 Oslo
www. touristbooks.com

Introduction:
Dr. Tom Bloch-Nakkerud
Design: Skomsøy Grønli AS
Translations: Berlitz GlobalNET
Printed in Denmark by Nørhaven AS

SFG

Also available:

DESTINATIONS COLLECTION

The Best of Norway

Languages:
English
German
French
Dutch
Portuguese
Chinese
Finnish
Norwegian
Italian
Spanish
Russian
Japanese
Korean

CLASSIC COLLECTION

Norway – incl. CD

Languages:
English
German
Spanish
Japanese
Norwegian
French
Italian
Russian

A Taste of Norway

Languages:
Norwegian
English
German
French

Th. Kittelsen: Trolls

Languages:
English
German
Spanish
Japanese
Norwegian
French
Italian
Dutch

HISTORY COLLECTION

The Vikings

Languages:
English
German
Italian
Spanish
Swedish
Icelandic
Norwegian
Japanese
French
Dutch
Danish
Russian

Viking Cookbook

Languages:
English
Spanish
Norwegian
German
French
Danish

SFG KIDS

Magnus Viking

Languages:
Norwegian
German
French
English
Spanish
Danish
Swedish

Elgar

Languages:
Norwegian
German
French
English
Spanish
Swedish

The Little Troll

Languages:
Norwegian
German
Spanish
Japanese
Swedish
English
French
Italian
Dutch

VIDEO COLLECTION

The Best of Norway

Format:	Languages:
VHS/PAL	English
VHS/NTSC	American
VHS/PAL	Norwegian
VHS/PAL	German
VHS/NTSC	Japanese
VHS/PAL	Italian
VHS/SECAM	French
VHS/PAL	Spanish
VHS/NTSC	Spanish
VHS/PAL	Korean

If your local retailer does not stock our titles, please visit our web site:
www.touristbooks.com